I used to be addicted to soap.

But I'm clean now

#1

I don't trust stairs.

They're always up to something

#2

Why was the math book
sad?

Because it had too many problems

#3

Dad, did you get a hair cut?

No, I got them all cut

#4

If you steal my computer, Ill
find you.

You have my Word.

#5

I wish I could be a doctor.

but I dont have the patients.

#6

What do you call an alligator in a vest?

An investigator!

What did the fish say when
it hit the wall?

Dam!

#8

Why did the tomato turn red?

Because it saw the salad dressing

#9

What side of a tree grows the most branches?

The outside!

When two vegans get in an argument,

is it still called a beef?

#11

Why do elephants never use computers?

They're afraid of the mouse

#12

Why couldn't the bicycle
stand up by itself?

Because it was two-tired

#13

How do you organize a space party?

You planet

#14

Why don't scientists trust atoms?

Because they make up everything

#15

What did the zero say to the eight?

Nice belt!

**#16

What gives you the power
to walk through a wall?

A door!

#17

What did one plate say to the other plate?

Dinner's on me!

#18

How do you make gold soup?

Put in 14 carrots

What do you call a sheep
with no legs?

A cloud

#20

How do you catch a squirrel?

Climb up in a tree and act like a nut

#21

What do you call a pile of cats?

A meowtain

#22

What do you call a pile of cats?

A meowtain

Why did the golfer bring two pairs of pants?

In case he got a hole in one!

#24

Why did the golfer bring two pairs of pants?

In case he got a hole in one!

#25

Why did the computer go to the doctor?

It had a virus!

#26

Why don't oysters give to charity?

Because they're shellfish

#27

Why did the banana go to the doctor?

Because it wasn't peeling well.

How does a penguin build its house?

Igloos it together

#29

www.ingramcontent.com/pod-product-compliance
Lightning Source LLC
Chambersburg PA
CBHW060949130726
48001CB00003B/1134